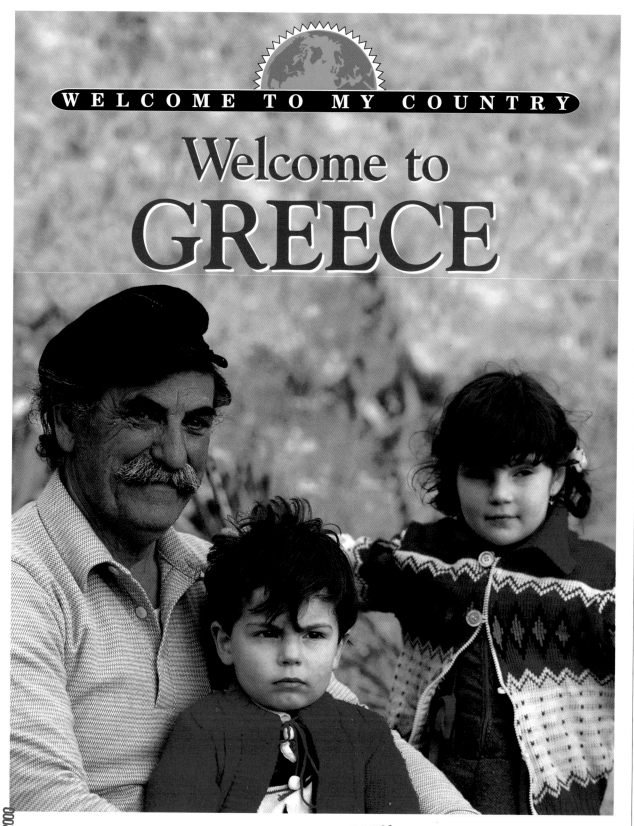

WELCOME TO MY COUNTRY

Welcome to
GREECE

Gareth Stevens Publishing
A WORLD ALMANAC EDUCATION GROUP COMPANY

Written by
NICOLE FRANK/YEOH HONG NAM

Designed by
LYNN CHIN

Picture research by
SUSAN JANE MANUEL

First published in North America in 2000 by
Gareth Stevens Publishing
A World Almanac Education Group Company
1555 North RiverCenter Drive, Suite 201
Milwaukee, Wisconsin 53212 USA

For a free color catalog describing
Gareth Stevens' list of high-quality books
and multimedia programs, call
1-800-542-2595 (USA) or
1-800-461-9120 (CANADA).
Gareth Stevens Publishing's
Fax: (414) 225-0377.

© **TIMES MEDIA PTE LTD 2000**
Originated and designed by
Times Editions Pte Ltd
An imprint of Times Media Private Limited
A member of the Times Publishing Group
Times Centre, 1 New Industrial Road
Singapore 536196
http://www.timesone.com.sg/te

Library of Congress Cataloging-in-Publication Data

Frank, Nicole.
Welcome to Greece / Nicole Frank and Yeoh Hong Nam.
p. cm. — (Welcome to my country)
Includes bibliographical references and index.
Summary: An overview of the country of Greece, discussing its
geography, history, government, economy, people, and culture.
ISBN 0-8368-2509-8 (lib. bdg.)
1. Greece—Juvenile literature. 2. Greece—Pictorial works—Juvenile
literature. [1. Greece.] I. Yeoh, Hong Nam. II. Title. III. Series.
DF30.F73   2000
949.5—dc21   99-058231

Printed in Malaysia

1 2 3 4 5 6 7 8 9 04 03 02 01 00

PICTURE CREDITS
A.N.A. Press Agency: 38
Giulio Andreini: 6, 18, 33 (bottom)
Archive Photos: 14, 17
Camera Press: 15 (center), 15 (bottom)
Bruce Coleman Collection: 3 (bottom),
  9 (bottom), 10
Sylvia Cordaiy Photo Library: 21, 23
Focus Team: 30, 41 (top)
Sonia Halliday: 32
Blaine Harrington: 4
HBL Network Photo Agency: 3 (center), 5, 7,
  31 (top)
Dave G. Houser Stock Photography: 16,
  31 (bottom)
The Hutchison Library: Cover, 1, 20, 24, 25, 34
The Image Bank: 41 (bottom)
Life File Photo Library: 28
North Wind Picture Archives: 15 (top), 29
Photobank Photolibrary: 3 (top), 26, 35
Pietro Scozzari: 2
Richard Shock/Silver Image Photo Agency: 43
David Simson: 37
Tom Till Photography: 8
Topham Picturepoint: 13, 19 (top), 36
Travel Ink: 9 (top), 11, 19 (bottom), 45
Trip Photographic Library: 12, 22, 27,
  33 (top), 39, 40

Digital Scanning by Superskill Graphics Pte Ltd

Contents

Words that appear in the glossary are printed in **boldface** type the first time they occur in the text.

Welcome to Greece!

Although Greece may be known for its rocky terrain, the country actually boasts a wide variety of scenery. The Greek landscape features fertile river basins, dense forests, and warm, sandy beaches. Let's learn all about Greece — its complex history, vibrant people, and incredible culture!

Opposite: Greek soldiers march in traditional uniforms at the Acropolis.

Below: Local women chat with tourists on the island of Kárpathos.

The Flag of Greece

The Greek flag consists of nine blue and white stripes and a white cross on a blue background. Blue represents the sky and sea, and white reflects Greece's fight for independence. The cross represents Greek Orthodox Christianity.

The Land

Greece, or the Hellenic Republic, sits on 50,949 square miles (131,958 square kilometers) of land. Eighty percent of the country is covered by mountains that run northwest to southeast. The sea cuts deep into the Greek mainland. Greece is bordered by Albania, the Former Yugoslav Republic of Macedonia, Bulgaria, and Turkey.

Below: The island of Crete is home to golden beaches and blue-green seas.

Islands and Volcanoes

The valleys and mountains of Greece were formed between 65 million and 1.7 million years ago. During this time, volcanic eruptions also created many new islands.

Today, Greece consists of three parts: the northern mainland, which connects Greece to the rest of Europe; the southern mainland; and the islands and archipelagos. The islands occupy 18 percent of the Greek territory.

Climate

Greece has a mild climate. Mountains in the north attract rain, and sea breezes make the coastal sun pleasant. Average summer temperatures hover around 80° Fahrenheit (27° Celsius), but heat waves occasionally bake the country.

Greek winters are wet, but temperatures rarely dip below 43°F (6°C). Mountains are capped with winter snow until spring.

Above: Delicate, yellow wildflowers blossom in front of rocks formed during a volcanic eruption many centuries ago.

Plants and Animals

Many types of trees and flowers, such as oaks, pines, firs, tulips, and irises, flourish in Greece. Some plants have developed into unique species.

Various animals, such as wildcats, deer, and jackals, make their home in Greece. Birds from northern Europe fly to Greece to escape the cold of winter.

Above: These purple bellflowers add a patch of color to the rocky slopes of Mt. Parnassus. Plants in Greece have adapted to the dry soil by growing fewer leaves and becoming shorter than similar plants in other countries.

Left: This rare lynx perches on a rock to survey its territory.

History

Greek history dates back nearly four thousand years, when the Minoan civilization was established in Crete. Through the centuries, the Greek navy and army sailed the Mediterranean Sea and invaded areas as far north as modern Russia.

During the fifth century B.C., Greece consisted of city-states. In 500 B.C., the Greek city-states defeated the Persians, who came from the Middle East.

Below: Tourists visit the ancient ruins of the Minoan palace of Knossos in Crete.

Macedonia and Byzantium

Around 350 B.C., King Philip II of Macedonia conquered the Greek city-states. His son, Alexander the Great, united Greece and expanded Greek civilization into Egypt, northern India, and Persian territories. In 146 B.C., Greece became part of the Roman Empire. When the empire split in two in A.D. 285, Greece became part of the eastern half of the Byzantine Empire, and Constantinople became its capital.

Above: An ancient Ionic column (*in the foreground*) and a Byzantine church (*in the middle*) blend into the architecture of modern Athens.

Left: A colorful tapestry shows the Turks' surrender in the Greek war of independence, which lasted from 1821 to 1829.

Independence and War

The Byzantine Empire was divided in the thirteenth century, and, in 1453, Constantinople fell to the Turkish-ruled Ottoman Empire. After centuries of **oppression**, the Greeks rebelled in 1821, and the Turks eventually granted Greece its independence in 1829.

In 1831, the first Greek president was **assassinated**, and **civil war** erupted. Many changes in government followed. In 1912, Italy attacked the Ottoman Empire and Greece seized many important territories from Turkey.

Greece participated in World War I (1914–1918) but failed to gain new territory. Italy and Germany invaded Greece during World War II (1939–1945), but Greece resisted and eventually defeated these powers.

Below: In 1941, German and Italian soldiers prepare for a victory parade in Athens.

Democracy Once More

The defeated German troops left Greece in 1945. Civil war loomed as the communists struggled for power. From 1949 to 1969, the United States provided Greece with money and arms to fight **communism**.

In 1967, the Greek military formed a **junta**, called "the colonels." In 1974, the junta collapsed, and Constantine Karamanlis began restoring democracy.

Below: Constantine Karamanlis (1907–1998) was Greece's prime minister from 1955 to 1963. He was influential in Greek politics during the 1970s and 1980s and was elected president in 1980 and 1990.

Solon (c. 630–530 B.C.)

Solon was the Athenian statesman who abolished slavery in Athens. He struggled for humane laws and fought against poverty. Solon was one of the Seven Wise Men of Greece.

Solon

Andreas Papandreou (1919–1996)

Andreas Papandreou left Greece when the colonels took power but later returned and founded the Panhellenic Socialist Movement (PASOK). In 1981, he was elected prime minister. He retired from politics in 1996.

Andreas Papandreou

Melina Mercouri (1925–1994)

The arts scene flourished under Melina Mercouri, the minister of culture appointed in 1981. She is best known for asking Britain to return to Greece the Elgin Marbles, sculptures once removed from the Parthenon.

Melina Mercouri

Government and the Economy

Government

Greece is a presidential republic. The basis for the current Greek constitution was formed when the colonels fell in 1974. The president is elected by the parliament to a five-year term, and he or she has only ceremonial powers. The *vouli* (VOO-li), or parliament, and the

Below:
The parliament building looks out over Constitution Square in Athens.

prime minister hold real power. The vouli consists of 300 members, who are elected to four-year terms by ballot.

Greece has thirteen regions, divided into fifty-one prefectures. The two major political parties are the Panhellenic Socialist Movement and the New Democratic Party.

Six percent of Greece's national budget is spent on defense. Greek men must serve in the military.

Above: Armed Greek soldiers guard the planes at an air base.

Economy

Greece has made economic progress in recent years, but it still falls behind other European countries. Shipping and tourism are Greece's main sources of income.

Historically, most Greeks prefer to be self-employed than to work for big companies. Greece's service industry now generates 60 percent of the national income. Today, fewer Greeks leave to work overseas.

Above:
Green grapes are harvested in Crete. A large variety of fruit is grown in Greece. This produce is sold locally and around the world.

Natural Resources

Fertile soil in Thessaly and in Eastern Macedonia and Thrace makes these regions important agricultural areas. Major crops include tomatoes, grain, sugar, cotton, olives, grapes, melons, oranges, and peaches. In recent years, the fishing industry has declined.

Above: Greek women examine containers of olives at a shop.

Food, steel, cement, and livestock are Greece's major exports. Greece trades mainly with other European countries, especially Germany and Italy.

Left: Vehicles unload from a ship at the port of Preveza in Epirus. Shipping is an important part of the Greek economy.

People and Lifestyle

The Hellenes

Greeks, who call themselves Hellenes, have preserved their language, culture, and identity, despite past invasions.

Today, Greece has a **homogeneous** population, with only 2 percent being **ethnic minorities**. Ninety-eight percent of the people belong to the Greek Orthodox Church.

Below: Two Greek children spend a day with their grandfather.

Muslims and Albanians

Muslims make up about 1 percent of the population and live in northeastern Greece. They are represented by at least four parliament members.

Albanians were brought into Greece to settle underpopulated areas in the 1100s. Today, their descendants consider themselves Greek. Recently, 300,000 Albanian refugee workers came to Greece and were given shelter and jobs.

Above: A Gypsy shopkeeper plays the guitar. Gypsies are a small minority in Greece.

Family

Greek families are close-knit. In the past, rural communities were very close because travel between villages was difficult. Modern urban life is more independent, but family remains a top priority.

In the past, Greek families gave their marrying daughters **dowries** to ensure that the newlyweds had a

Below: Christmas and other holidays are times for extended families to get together and celebrate.

22

comfortable life. Today, this system is no longer used. The government abolished the practice in the early 1980s, and many women are now financially independent. Today, Greek women are free to choose whether to have a job, a family, or both.

Above: These men enjoy a leisurely afternoon at a local cafe. In conservative Greek communities, men and women have separate social groups and activities.

Greek children are given two godparents, or ***nonos*** (noh-NOS), at birth. Godparents are responsible for a child's spiritual life and often give financial and emotional support, too.

Education

Ancient Greece produced many famous thinkers. Education is still a priority today. From the ages of six to twelve, children attend primary school, then spend three years at middle school, or *gymnasium* (jim-NAH-see-um). High school, or *lyceum* (lee-SEE-um), follows.

Public education is free, but many students take additional classes at private schools.

Further Education

Competition to enter a university is tough because schools are few in number. Today, secure jobs in the city, which often require university diplomas, attract many young people from the countryside.

The government has addressed its education shortage by improving schools and building new universities. Many students also participate in foreign exchange programs.

Below: These university students stop to chat between classes.

Religion

In 1850, the Greek Orthodox Church became independent of Constantinople. Although the Church is self-governed, it recognizes the Ecumenical Patriarch in Istanbul as its spiritual leader.

Ten million Greeks belong to the Church. Greece is divided into eighty-one dioceses, or religious districts, run

Above: This abbot (*arms raised*) participates in the **Niptras** (nip-TRAS) before Good Friday. During this ceremony, priests reenact Jesus Christ's washing of his disciples' feet before the Last Supper.

by Orthodox bishops. Orthodox priests are active in community life and take part in many religious ceremonies.

Greek Muslims, Roman Catholics, Protestants, and Jews account for only 2 percent of the Greek population.

Monasteries

Monasteries have helped shape Greek spiritual life for about one thousand years. Some monks live secluded lives, while others are part of communities. Today, fewer and fewer people choose the monastic life.

Below: The isolated Meteora monasteries sit high atop the Pindus Mountains in Thessaly.

Language

Talk to Me

Greek, in one form or another, has been used for more than three thousand years. It was the language of the Gospels and has contributed to all Western languages. In the third century, *dimotiki* (dee-moh-tee-KEE) was the spoken Greek dialect. In the 1830s, a new language, called *katharévousa* (kah-thah-REH-voo-sah), was created. It was very hard to learn, however, and in 1975, dimotiki became the official language.

Below: Both Greek and English are used on signs in Athens.

A Good Story

Homer, a Greek poet, wrote the *Iliad*, one of the world's most famous ancient stories. It recounts the war between the Greeks and the city of Troy. Other famous ancient Greek writers include Sophocles and Euripides.

Modern Greek writers George Seferis and Odysseus Elytis won the Nobel Prize for literature in 1963 and 1979 respectively. Another modern Greek author, Níkos Kazantzakís, had two of his novels made into movies.

Arts

Art through the Ages

Greek art has awed the world for centuries. Builders in the geometric period (1100–700 B.C.) favored simple lines. Temple ruins in Crete and Sparta are examples of this architectural style.

During the archaic period (700–500 B.C.), Greeks incorporated Egyptian stone columns and carvings into their

Below: Ancient Greeks visited the temple of Delphi to consult the **Oracle** of Apollo on private and political matters.

work. Human figures began to look more lifelike. Marble became a favored building material during this period.

During the classical period (500–323 B.C.), the Greek city-states tried to outdo each other, building temples in the Doric, Ionic, and Corinthian architectural styles.

Builders used elements of Asian art and architecture during the Hellenistic period (from 323 B.C.).

From Icons to Landscapes

Only fragments of early paintings survive, but religious icons from the Byzantine period have been preserved. Many icons depict Jesus Christ or the Virgin Mary with the infant Jesus. From the fifteenth to the nineteenth centuries, Italian Renaissance art influenced artists on the Ionian Islands. Modern Greek paintings depict landscapes and people.

Above: Biblical characters painted during the twelfth century decorate the walls of a church in Cyprus.

Opposite: Plays have been staged at the Theater of Dionysus in Athens since the fifth century B.C.

All the World Is a Stage

Classical Greek drama was not just entertaining; it also gave the audience a moral lesson. Both comedies and dramas demonstrated the beliefs and values of Greek society. Greek drama has greatly influenced many famous writers, such as William Shakespeare.

Above: Traditional Greek actors wear stylized masks during dramatic productions.

During the classical period, plays were staged in open-air amphitheaters, where actors wore masks. Excellent **acoustics** allowed those sitting far away to hear the actors perfectly.

Leisure

Greece's warm climate lets people enjoy the outdoors throughout the year. City-dwellers participate in exercise, go to parks, and walk their dogs. Greek children enjoy card games and soccer.

In rural areas, people visit each other and host parties. Women make handicrafts, which they hang in their sitting rooms. Other popular pastimes include sculpture, reading, and writing.

Left: Boys play a game of cards in Cyprus.

Let's Celebrate!

Music, singing, and dancing are popular at Greek celebrations, such as Christmas and Easter. Guitarists and drummers play lively music, and people sing folk songs at every occasion. Colorfully dressed dancers also perform during festivals. Greek folk dances range from the festive and happy to the serious and solemn.

Above: Greek folk dancers perform at a festival.

Sports

The prestigious Olympic Games began in ancient Greece. Today, the country is home to amateur and professional athletes. Greek competitors in both wrestling and sailing have won Olympic medals.

Podosphero (poh-DOHS-fay-roh), or soccer, is Greece's national sport. The eighteen-team Greek soccer league plays games on Sunday, and excited spectators fill the stands to watch.

The Great Outdoors

Greeks love to relax in the great outdoors. Skiing, hunting, and auto racing are all popular pastimes. The clear, blue waters of the Greek islands attract locals and tourists alike. These islands provide a perfect setting for water sports, including fishing, sailing, boating, and waterskiing. The clear waters also let swimmers and divers observe marine life.

Below: Fresh lobsters are served to tourists at a seaside restaurant in Kérkira.

Holidays

Pascha (PAHS-kah), or Easter, is the most important day in the Greek Orthodox calendar. The carnival season takes place during the three weeks before Lent. On Holy Saturday, processions leave churches at midnight to reenact the search for Christ's body. Dressed in their finest clothes, people feast and have fun after attending church on Easter Sunday.

Below: During Easter, women on the island of Kárpathos wear colorful, traditional dress with necklaces of gold coins to symbolize wealth.

Above: Students and soldiers march through the streets on Ochi Day.

Independence Day, celebrated on March 25, marks the end of four hundred years of Turkish rule in Greece. Greece eventually gained independence in 1829, after an eight-year war.

During World War II, Greek prime minister Ioánnis Metaxas replied, "*Ochi* (o-HEE)," or "No," when Italy asked to occupy Greece. Ochi Day on October 28 celebrates Greek pride.

Food

The first cookbook in history was written in 330 B.C. by Greek Archestratos. Today, Greek cuisine has adopted ideas and flavors from the Middle East and Western Europe.

Simplicity, fresh ingredients, herbs and spices, and olive oil form the basis of good Greek food. Vegetables are

Below: An Easter Sunday feast is a good opportunity for the members of a large Greek family to get together.

fresh and tasty because Greece's sunny Mediterranean climate is very suitable for herbs and vegetables.

Greeks love seafood and lamb. Favorite dishes include *kalamari* (kah-lah-MAH-ree), or squid, and *souvlaki* (soov-LAH-kee), or barbecued lamb kebabs. Fresh fruit and pastries are popular desserts.

Food and **hospitality** are important to Greek culture. Good cooks are well respected by friends and family.

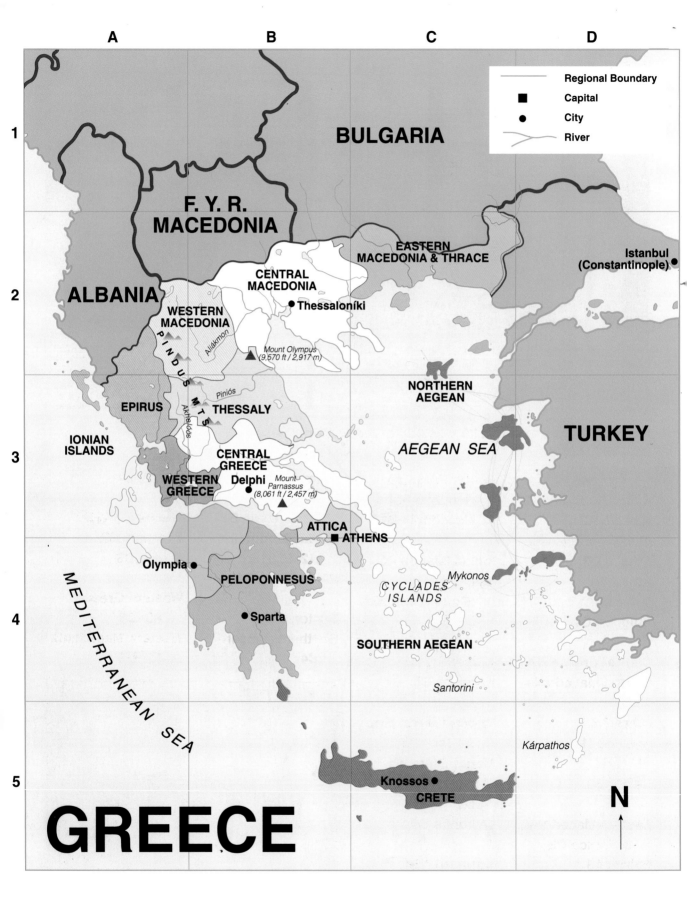

GREECE

Above: Boats cruise in a lake on one of the Santorini islands.

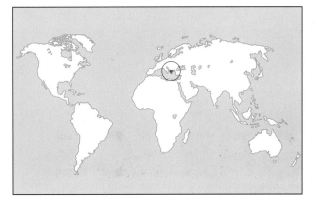

Quick Facts

Official Name	The Hellenic Republic
Capital	Athens
Official Language	Greek
Population	10,565,000 (1998 estimate)
Land Area	50,949 square miles (131,958 square km)
Regions	Attica, Central Greece, Central Macedonia, Crete, Eastern Macedonia and Thrace, Epirus, Ionian Islands, Northern Aegean, Peloponnesus, Southern Aegean, Thessaly, Western Greece, Western Macedonia
Highest Point	Mount Olympus (9,570 feet/2,917 m)
Major Rivers	Aliákmon, Akhelöós, Piniós
Official Religion	Greek Orthodox Christianity
Famous Leaders	Alexander the Great
	Elefthérios Venizélos
	Constantine Karamanlis
	Andreas Papandreou
Important Holidays	Pascha, or Easter; Independence Day; Ochi Day
Currency	Drachma (Grd 280 = U.S. $1 in 1999)

Opposite: The island of Mykonos has an unusual mascot — Petros the pelican!

Glossary

acoustics: the features of a room or theater that determine how clearly sounds are heard in it.

assassinated: murdered for political or religious reasons.

civil war: a war between two groups from the same country.

communism: a system of government based on the common ownership of property.

dimotiki (dee-moh-tee-KEE): demotic Greek, a commonly spoken form of the Greek language.

dowries: the items a woman brings to her husband when she gets married.

ethnic minorities: racial or national groups that make up small parts of the population.

gymnasium (jim-NAH-see-um): a secondary school for young people aged thirteen to fifteen.

homogeneous: all the same kind.

hospitality: being nice and welcoming to guests in your home.

junta: a small group ruling a country, especially after a coup and before a legal government has been instituted.

kalamari (kah-lah-MAH-ree): squid.

katharévousa (kah-thah-REH-voo-sah): "pure" Greek, a form of Greek that is close to ancient Greek.

lyceum (lee-SEE-um): an institution that students attend from age sixteen.

Niptras (nip-TRAS): the washing ceremony before Good Friday that reenacts Jesus Christ's washing of his disciples' feet before the Last Supper.

nonos (noh-NOS): a godparent.

ochi (o-HEE): no

oppression: the state of being subdued and kept down through harsh and cruel use of power or authority.

oracle: a shrine or temple at which requests are made to a deity (god) and divine answers conveyed through a medium or priest.

Pascha (PAHS-kah): Easter.

podosphero (poh-DOHS-fay-roh): soccer.

replica: a copy or duplicate.

souvlaki (soov-LAH-kee): grilled or barbecued pieces of lamb on skewers.

vouli (VOO-li): the Greek parliament.

More Books to Read

Alexander the Great. Ancient Biographies series. Robert Green (Franklin Watts)

Ancient Greeks. Worldwise series. Daisy Kerr (Franklin Watts)

Athens. Cities of the World series. Conrad R. Stein (Children's Press)

Daily Life. Ancient Greece series. Stewart Ross (Peter Bedrick Books)

Greece. The Ancient World series. Robert Hill (Raintree/Steck Vaughn)

Greece. Festivals of the World series. Efstathia Sioras (Gareth Stevens)

Greece: The Culture. Lands, Peoples, and Cultures series. Sierra Adare (Crabtree Publishing)

The Original Olympics. Stewart Ross (Peter Bedrick Books)

Science in Ancient Greece. Kathlyn Gay (Franklin Watts)

We Goddesses: Athena, Aphrodite, Hera. Doris Orgel (DK Publishing)

Videos

Ancient Greece: Volumes 1 and 2. (Kultur Video)

Greece. (IVN Entertainment)

Greece. (Time-Life Video)

Greece: Athens and the Peloponnes, Greek Islands. (Questar Inc.)

Web Sites

www.greekembassy.org/

www.odci.gov/cia/publications/ factbook/gr.html

www.odysseas.com/history.html

www.lausd.k12.ca.us/lausd/history/ greece/

Due to the dynamic nature of the Internet, some web sites stay current longer than others. To find additional web sites about Greece, use a reliable search engine and enter one or more of the following keywords: *Alexander the Great, Athens, Cyprus, Greek-Americans, Olympic Games, Parthenon, Zákinthos.*

Index